NATIONAL GEOGRAPHIC

T0045499

Zoo Map

David Tunkin

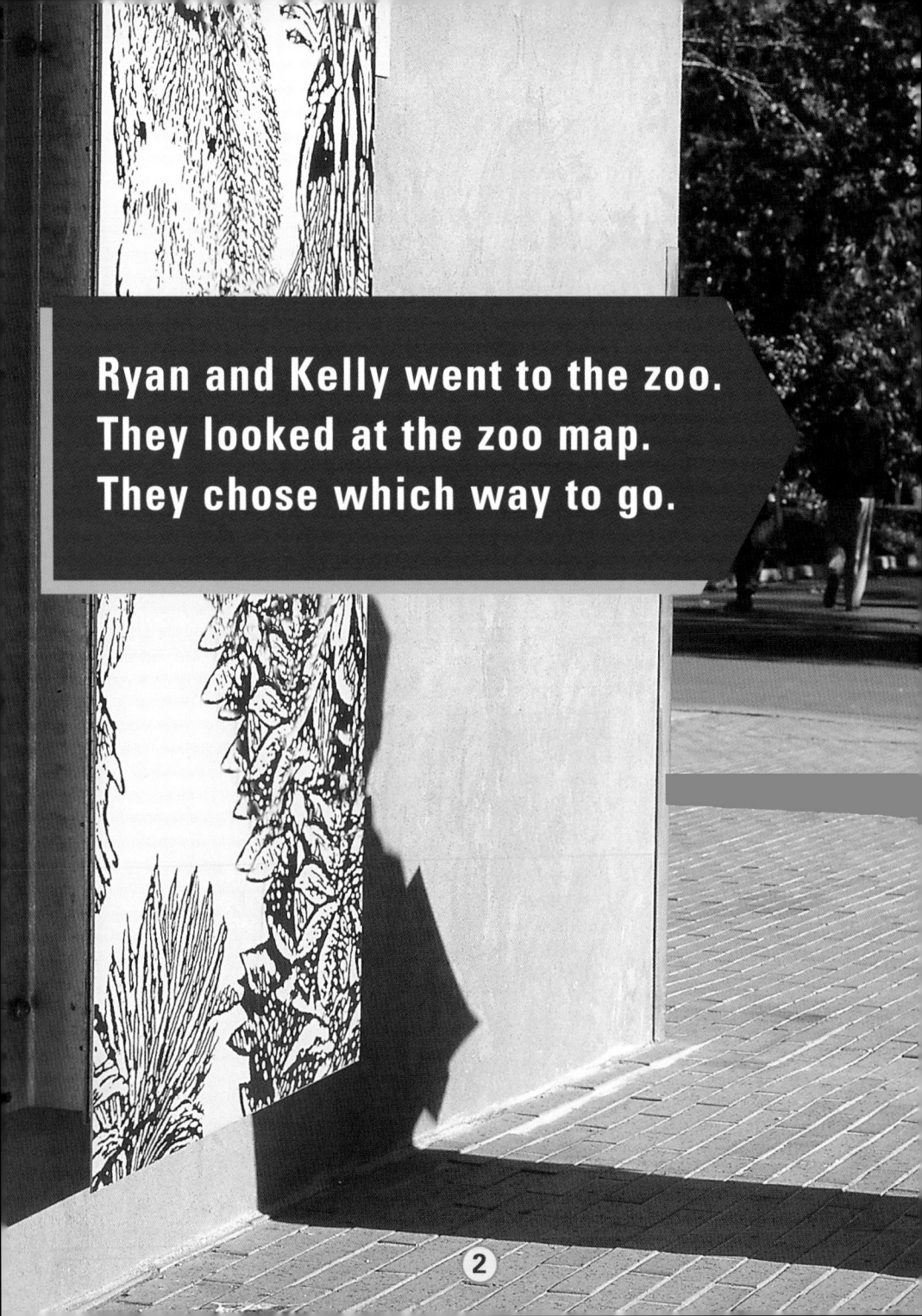

Ryan and Kelly went to the zoo.
They looked at the zoo map.
They chose which way to go.

way!
Entrance
ZOO

To Lions
Seals
To Kangaroos
Tigers
Lions

Seals
To Kangaroos

Alligators
Kangaroos
To Bears
Flamingoes
Hippos

Ryan and Kelly went to see the bears. What did they see on the way?

Which animals do you like to see at the zoo?
Open the page to see the zoo map.

Look at the zoo map.
Can you find your way to see these animals?
How would you get there?
Entrance
ZOO
To Lions
Tigers
Lions
Seals
To Kangaroos
Alligators

Kangaroos
Elephants
Zoo Exit
To Bears
Flamingoes
Hippos
Bears
Vultures
Monkeys
Zebras

Picture Glossary

Alligators

Bears

Elephants

Flamingoes

Hippos

Kangaroos

Lions

Monkeys

Seals

Tigers

Vultures

Zebras